Sinbad
and the Roc

retold by Ian Whybrow

illustrated by Nick Schon

CAMBRIDGE
UNIVERSITY PRESS

UCL
Institute of Education

Once upon a time, there was a man
called Sinbad.

He loved to go to faraway lands
and find treasure.

Now you might think that Sinbad was rich.

But he gave his treasure away to anyone
who was poor.

2

One day, he found he had nothing left.

Sinbad was not upset.

'I need to find more treasure,' he cried.

'It's time for another adventure!'

Sinbad went down to the seashore.

He needed a big ship to sail to faraway lands.

He found some sailors who wanted to go with him.

The sailors packed the ship with plenty of food and plenty of water.

Soon they were ready to leave.

At first, the sea was calm
and the sun was shining.

But soon a great storm blew up.

The ship was tossed about on the waves.

All of the food and water was washed
into the sea.

The sailors were very worried.

Sinbad was not worried.

'Cheer up, lads!' he said to the sailors.

'I can see an island up ahead.

Maybe we can get food to eat and
water to drink.

Let's go and see what we can find.'

Sinbad rowed to the island.

He started climbing a hill to look around the island.

He didn't see the giant bird flying overhead.

It had an enormous snake in its beak.

But the sailors had seen it!

'Help! It's a Roc!' one of the sailors yelled.
'It will kill us all!'

The sailors were scared.

They sailed away from the island
as fast as they could.

Soon, Sinbad got to the top of the hill and looked around.

He could see sticks – lots of sticks.

This wasn't an island. This was a nest.

And it wasn't a hill that he had climbed.

It was the Roc's egg!

The sky above him began to grow darker.

The Roc was going to land right
on top of Sinbad!

Sinbad could hear the sound
of munching and crunching.

What could it be?

He peeped out from under the Roc's feathers.

The Roc was eating an enormous snake.

Now you might think that Sinbad was scared.

But he was not.

He had seen something sparkling
on the snake's skin.

'Diamonds!' thought Sinbad.

'That's just what I came for.'

Now all he needed was a plan.

Sinbad took off his turban and tied himself to the Roc's leg.

Then he waited.

Next morning, the Roc was hungry again.

She flew off over the sea to a deep valley.

Sinbad held on tight.

The Roc dived down to get a snake
for her breakfast.

The Roc grabbed a fat snake.

'This snake is very sticky,' said Sinbad
to himself, 'and it is covered in diamonds!'

He quickly untied himself.

This time he made his turban into a bag.

He filled it full of diamonds.

Then he ran away as fast as he could.

When he got to the sea, Sinbad met some merchants with a big ship.

'Will you take me back to my home?' he asked them.

'Yes, if you can pay us,' they said.

'I can pay you with diamonds!'
Sinbad said with a smile.

When he got home, he told everyone
about his adventure.

The king sent for Sinbad to hear the story
of the Roc for himself.

'These are for you, sir,' said Sinbad,
and he gave the king some diamonds.

The king was very pleased.

Now you might think that Sinbad
stayed at home, happy with his diamonds.

And he did ...

... until it was time for another adventure!

Sinbad and the Roc ❧ Ian Whybrow

Teaching notes written by Sue Bodman and Glen Franklin

Using this book

Developing reading comprehension

This is a retelling of the second of the seven voyages of Sinbad. It wil be helpful if the children have already read the first voyage 'Sinbad Goes to Sea' earlier in the Cambridge Reading Adventures (Turquoise band). The character of Sinbad is developed through his behaviour, dialogue and action. A series of events build over time to a resolution, which is left open ready for Sinbad's next adventure.

Grammar and sentence structure

- Adverbial phases signal the passing of time ('At first; 'But soon).
- Sentence structure is varied for literary effect, for example: 'He could see sticks – lots of sticks.' (page 10).

Word meaning and spelling

- Language structures follow elements of traditional retellings, such as the use of 'Once Upon a Time' to open the story, and in vocabulary choices: 'to faraway lands' (page 4).
- Some novel, context-specific vocabulary is introduced, such as 'merchants' and 'treasure' for which children will need to use effective word reading strategies including breaking words into known chunks.

Curriculum links

Science – A Roc is a mythical creature but it has the features of a bird of prey. Children could use non-fiction texts and information on websites to find out about real birds of prey and write their own non-fiction reports. They could innovate on the genre to create imaginary reports about Rocs.

Art - The illustrator has drawn his interpretation of what he thinks a Roc may look like. Ask the children to draw or paint their idea of a Roc referring to photographs of birds of prey, or pictures of other mythical creatures for support.

Learning Outcomes

Children can:

- read at a greater pace, sometimes silently
- compare the story features with those of other traditional tales
- use the language of time to discuss story sequence
- solve novel, unfamiliar words using appropriate reading strategies.

A guided reading lesson

Book Introduction

Discuss what is known already of Sinbad (that he likes adventures, that he likes helping people, that he gives all his money away). Give each child a book and read the title to them. *In this new Sinbad story he is off on another adventure. This time he meets a Roc. What do you think a Roc could be?* Point out the shadow of the big bird on the front cover, if the children fail to see it. Read the back cover blurb together. Say: *Oh, yes – it says that he meets a giant bird. You were right.*

Preparation

Page 2: Ask the children to read the first line with you: *'Once upon a time'.* Say: *Do you know other stories that start like that? What sort of stories are they? I wonder if this will be the same sort of story.* Remind the children how Sinbad got his treasure in his previous adventure, but now it is all spent.

Pages 4 and 5: Look at the use of literary language such as *'faraway lands'* and the impact of repetition for effect: *'plenty of*